CONTENT MARKETING-REBOOT

How to Win Clients and Influence Markets

DR(HC) RAECHELLE RAE JOHNSON

Copyright by Dr(hc) Raechelle Rae Johnson All rights reserved

No part of this publication may be reproduced, stored or transmitted in any form or by any means, electronic, mechanical, photocopying, recording, scanning, or otherwise without written permission from the publisher. It is illegal to copy this book, post it to a website, or distribute it by any other means without permission. © 2022

ACKNOWLEDGEMENTS

Thank you to my biggest cheerleaders; my boys, my son, and nephew-son, for believing I can do anything I want to try. To my two good, good girlfriends, +1, and big brother, Pastor/Friend/Sister, Celeste Whitley; confident, Alisha; Accountability Partner/Assistant (etc), my angel and forever plus one, Toni Perkins, and Pastor/Friend/Big Brother, Randy Whitley.

To my family (who doesn't always know what I am doing but are always ready to ride). To my second pair of eyes, project manager, and the woman who has made this project possible, Coach Tia Monique of Let It Out Academy™. To each of you for your interest, trust, and continuous support.

PREFACE

Content creation doesn't have to be difficult; yet sometimes it is. It's the one thing so many businesses struggle with. It's the thing that prevents a large number of businesses from:

- Achieving and maintaining their objective.
- Increasing their revenue and advancing to the next level.
- Amazing launches and selling out all spots.

Here's the deal: A few informative tidbits here and there won't help attract clients or keep your current ones. Promoting whenever or however you want won't provide you the steady 5/6 figure months you want. Without a viable Content Market Strategy, you won't be able to achieve your significant business goals.

What should you do? Show up regularly with high-value material to separate yourself apart from the crowd. STOP creating information that is searchable on Google. Take a fresh approach, give your narrative, and provide new ideas and recommendations to pique people's interest in you, your business, your products, and your services.

In this crowded industry, *"Content Marketing Strategy - Reboot, How to Win Clients and Influence Markets"* will provide you with the tools and knowledge you need to stand out in every manner and design a content marketing plan that establishes you as an expert and converts more dream clients.

Table of Contents

Table of Contents

ACKNOWLEDGEMENTS i
PREFACE.. ii
Table of Contents iii
WHAT IS CONTENT STRATEGY?... 1
CREATING "CONTENT MARKETINGSTRATEGY" 6
   STEP 1 The GOAL 8
   STEP 2 8
   STEP 3 12
   STEP 4 14
   STEP 5 18
   STEP 6 19
   STEP 7 25
   STEP 8 28
   OPTIMIZE YOUR SOCIAL PERSONA 34
   Select A Professional Username 34
   High-Quality Profile Photo 35
   A Compelling "About" Section 35
   Professional Cover Photo 36
   Your Contact Information 37
   Professionalism 37
   Use Hashtags 37
AWARENESS & VISIBILITY 40

Engage With Your Followers 43
Follow The Right People 45
DISTRIBUTION AND MARKETING 47
Owned Media Channels 48
Earned Media Channels 49
Paid Distribution Channels 50
SEO 51
PUTTING IT ALL TOGETHER 53
DON'T WAIT ANY LONGER! 54
Growing Your Business Using Social Media 57
Everything You Need to Know 58

1st PRINCIPLE

WHAT IS CONTENT STRATEGY?

Whether you are just starting out with content marketing, or you have been using the identical approach for ages, it never hurts to revisit your content marketing strategy plan to make sure it is up-to-date, innovative, and interesting for your customers. Content is the foundation of your brand, and how you structure this content affects how you deliver it to your current and potential customers. If you develop an efficient strategy for creating content, supported by a comprehensive understanding of your audience, you'll not only drive leads but increase sales as well. Unlike other advantage generation strategies, content marketing offers something to prospective clients, rather than asking them for something. Since 60% of e-Marketers create a minimum of one piece of content per day, you have your work cut out for you. However, it's more than worth it – by developing and promoting the correct content to the correct audience, you'll grow your traffic to over 200% in under 30 days.

Content strategy is the piece of your marketing plan that continuously demonstrates the "who". It helps to establish you as the expert (or thought leader). Focus on creating valuable, relevant, and consistent content across multiple channels that attract (and retain) your audience. You might have heard how important content creation is to the expansion of your business, but as you'll see throughout your reading, a well-planned content strategy can ensure your efforts translate into tangible results.

Don't forget that this can be accomplished with no budget, zero connection, and in your spare time. You are not reinventing the wheel; the data is obtainable if you know where to look; make it yours and put in the work. Yup, this is a job for YOU! After reading this book, you'll have the practical steps to form your own content marketing strategy. It is up to you to define your success.

This strategy, known as "Content Marketing Strategy", is a high-level approach for creating and marketing content. The focused approach for creating content includes topic selection, content formats, writing style, designs, and promotions. I repeat, whether you are just starting out with content marketing, or you've been using the same tactics for a while, it never hurts to revisit your strategy—to make sure it's up-to-date, innovative, and engaging for your current and potential clients.

Are you having trouble planning or in need of fresh ideas to include in your plan? Content Marketing Strategy, How to Win Clients and Influence Markets provides the right information and resources to set you out on a productive Content Marketing path. We will dive deeper into the meaning of content 'marketing, explore the vital strategy you must employ, examine the relevance of a content marketing plan to your business in the process of winning your ideal clients and influencing your target markets, with the steps needed to create your strategy.

In the competitive marketing landscape, the top benefit of Content Marketing is that it is crucial to the [business'] mission-critical growth method, most effective in growing audience engagement, developing your brand presence, and driving sales. You can build trust with your audience, connect with the clients, generate leads and improve conversions; not to mention establish your credibility and strengthen your reputation.

When you develop a content strategy, there are some areas to focus on: Who is your audience? What is your USP (unique selling position)? What is the problem you'll solve? What channel(s) will you focus on? How will you manage your content?

Marketers need to strategize their content to ensure it meets the pre-defined Key Performance Indicators (KPIs) and supports the company's business and financial goals which often include raising brand awareness, establishing oneself as an industry influencer, generating leads, or increasing sales. A well-defined content strategy will close the gap between your marketing KPIs and actual results. This gives you the most out of your content.

Ready to establish an online presence, attract audience engagement, validate your expertise, generate leads, and convert followers/users to sales or improve your rankings? Once you have defined your goal and the measured steps to reach them, you want to research your audience and focus on your USP. You receive the best bang for your hard-earned time when you know who gains from your content and where they are showing up already. This also helps you to narrow down the most favorable marketing mix for those audiences on any given channel. Statistically, most individuals organically won't see 97.7% of the content available online. To avoid being a part of this statistic, choose relevant content that stands out.

A strong content strategy considers the KPIs and works towards reaching them. It's a roadmap that involves planning out each step that needs to be taken to reach each objective, the overarching goal.

The very thought of creating a content strategy can be overwhelming but consider the content strategy as your marketing goal blueprint.

Key Performance Indicators – every business has its own personality; therefore, it's essential to track KPIs that are relevant to growing your brand. Focus, you want to know if your marketing efforts are effective. Don't spend unnecessary time, energy or money doing what isn't driving results.

Great content strategy doesn't just happen. It needs complete methodical planning, attention to detail, and precise execution. However, the sooner you start, the sooner you'll have your strategy up, running, and closer to achieving your KPIs goal [see the KPI Template on page 5].

There is a large population of prominent organization marketers using content marketing. In fact, content marketing is a strategic marketing approach focused on creating and distributing valuable, relevant, and consistent content to drive profitable customer action. It is used by leading brands to attract and retain their target audience. Content Marketing is good for your bottom line. This is because it works!

Let's dive into the specifics of creating your strategic plan.

CONTENT KPI

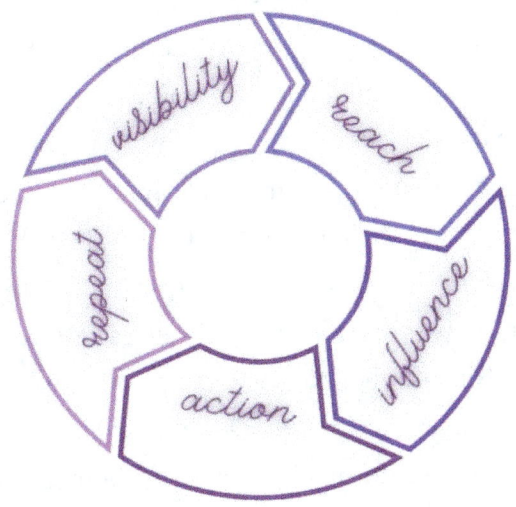

in-process

Reach [%] of population
Keep share of voice at [%]

Reach [%] of people
showing some comment intent

Add [%] referral traffic from [#] of social
medical multi-mediums

Reach [%] of people
showing some comment intent

Reach [%] of existing customers

output-process

Grow top-of-mind-awareness (toma) by +[%]

Grow branded searches by +[%]

Streamline content marketing strategy by [%]
and target [%] of market

Grow topline revenue by +[%] at [%] profitability

Get [%] of existing customers to repeat purchase

2nd PRINCIPLE

CREATING "CONTENT MARKETING STRATEGY"

Content strategy refers to the management of any tangible media that you create and own: written, visual, or downloadable. It implies the piece of your marketing plan that continuously demonstrates the "who". It helps to establish you as the expert (or thought leader), and focus on creating valuable, relevant, and consistent content across multiple channels that attract (and retain) your audience. You might have heard how important content creation is to the expansion of your business, but as you will see throughout your reading, it must have a well-planned purpose.

When you develop a content strategy, there are some areas to focus on: Who is your audience? What is your USP (Unique Selling Position)? What is the problem you'll solve? What channel(s) will you focus on? How will you manage your content?

Your content should cover the three basic principles. The first principle is awareness. This helps your client or audience to consider the content in the place. It must be predicated on a format that proves appealing to them. The second principle is evaluation. This takes them on a journey that arrives at the place of results via a range of soft to strong calls to action using brand penetration, brand strategy and key principles. Finally, conversion creates audience satisfaction and advocacy, a relation of the network community. So, let us revisit some earlier terms and how they play a role in content strategy. A strong content marketing strategy requires a solid framework.

7 STEPS TO CREATE A SOLID FRAME FOR A STRONG CONTENT MARKETING STRATEGY

Detailed goals and KIPs can be tracked and measured. An in-depth content calendar provides a visual map of scheduled content that will make it easier to manage. A variety of content types will capture interest and audience intrigue (i.e. posts, infographics, videos, eBooks, podcasts, etc.). Content channels maximize the exposure of content to target audience(s). The right marketing and automation tools can be used to automate various processes of your marketing efforts. Copywriters, graphic designers, and video editors will help in creating high-quality readable, visually appealing and inviting content for a specific audience(s) in targeted markets. It is also important to budget. Content marketing is an investment created to generate leads and revenue. Your budget creates room to actualize content marketing strategy.

Your content strategy should include some basic elements. One of your priorities is to define your goal(s). Are you creating content to establish an online presence, attract audience engagement, validate your expertise, generate leads, convert followers/users to sales, or improve your rankings? This must be spelled out to precisely invest your time, resources, and energy most productively.

STEP 1

The GOAL

Your goals? With every client, we go over the Ultimate Branding Guide. Before completion, you'll learn what to do and how your plan will benefit your product/service. What is your aim for developing a content marketing plan? Why do you want to provide content and makes a content marketing plan? Know your goals before you start planning and you may have a more seamless time determining what is best for your strategy. To define your goals, ask yourself these questions: Who are you? What do you do? Why do you do it? How do you sell the pain and solve the product/service? What is your unique selling position? What are your short and long-term goals? How will content marketing help?

What matters to you? The one thing that means the most; that which connects your 'why' to the client's desired outcome through process. When focused, purpose has the power to shape priority which gives clarity in all communication via your content marketing planning.

STEP 2

Your One Thing

Once you have defined your goal and the measured steps to reach them, you want to research your audience and focus on your USP. You receive the best bang for your hard-earned time when you know who gains from your content and where they are showing up already. Note; this also helps you to narrow down the most favorable marketing mix for those audiences on any given channel. Statistically, most individuals organically won't see 97.7% of the content available online. To avoid being a part of these statistics, choose relevant content that stands out.

Raechelle-ism, relevant—purposeful, beneficial (or evergreen), unique and integral. How do we distinguish these elements for our audience based on our USP? It's quite simple. Listen to them, your market, your network, and your audience.

We will dive deeper in a moment into who your target audience is and what your USP is. Once you have decided what your focus will be on and on whom, listen to what ails and aids them. This is their pain point(s) and this is what they need. And here lies your why. Pain points are specific problems faced by current or prospective customers in the marketplace. This gives you a clear black and white picture of what your content should be. Now, amplify your content.

Consumers can easily become overwhelmed with options, and a quick understanding of what makes one product or brand different from another is imperative to their decision-making. It is important to also know the right way to position yourself and your products. It is the difference between standing out and blending in. That's why you must understand how to identify a unique selling proposition (USP) to help guide your branding and marketing decisions.

Your competitors have an analogous product to yours, which suggests your potential customers must know what makes yours better — or, at least, different. Here's where content comes in. So, to prove why you are worth buying from, you must prove why you are worth paying attention to.

Ideally, your product or service solves an issue you recognize your audience has. By the identical token, your content coaches and educates your audience through this problem as they start to spot and address it. *"When we quit thinking primarily about ourselves and our self-preservation, we undergo a truly heroic transformation of our consciousness to do something bigger than ourselves" – Joseph Campbell.*

The Hero's/Heroine's Journey [See the Hero's Journey example on page 12] allows the reader to find themselves in the identity of your brand, adopt then adapt, giving themselves permission to build trust in the foundation of the relationship. "There's no revenue without trust".

- The want (or Call – Awareness)
- Departure (or Challenge – Interest)
- Listens to advisers (or Transformation – Desire)
- Going for the goal
- The Decision Decides (Twist – Doubt/Trust)
- Succeeds/Fail (Resolution – Action)
- Onboarding (Brand Loyalty).

To further simplify the steps of this cycle consider using the 3 Act Structure.

We've been telling stories for longer than we've been writing them down. The three-act story structure was employed long beforewe had a name for this storytelling technique.

The three-act structure is one of the best ways to ensure your story structure is made for those you want to create a strong and authentic connection with. If you're learning how to construct a story or simplywant to ensure your story structure is made for those you want to create a strong and authentic connection with, using it is one of the best ways to do so.

This strategy is still used by very successful and well-known auditors today.

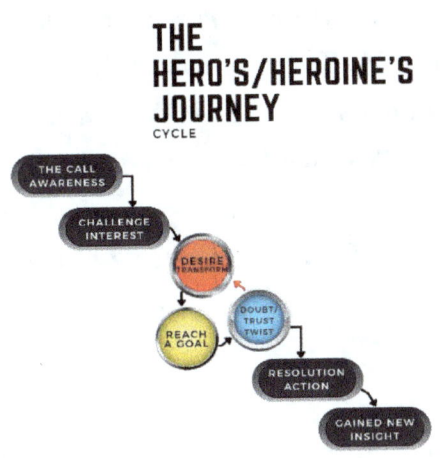

What is your aim for developing a content marketing plan? Why do you want to provide content and make a content marketing plan? Know your goals before you start planning and you can have a seamless time determining what is best for your strategy.

Remember, to develop a success plan, you obviously must define your content's audience — also called your buyer persona.

If you are an experienced marketer, your target may have changed. You now get to decide if you want to focus on a replacement group of individuals or expand your current target market. Either way, revisiting your audience parameters by conducting marketing research every year is crucial to growing your audience.

Start by ensuring you have clear goals and objectives. You must decide what you wish to accomplish with your social media campaign. Whether it is increasing brand exposure, driving leads, or earning conversions, you must be aware of your end goal.

Your strategy should specialize in growing your business' presence and achieving measurable results. You must specialize in objectives that you will be able to monitor to make sure that you are driving success along with your campaign.

Raechelle-ism – G.O.A.T., What is your overarching desire (GOAL). Strategically placed OBJECTIVES on how you will measure your goals for desired results. Calculated steps, ACTIONS will assist you in creating the daily/weekly TASKS needed to measure your objectives at each junction where you expect to see the results that lead to your desired goal(s). [Visit Linktr.ee/theSolutionArchitect for a Goal Template]

STEP 3

Establish Your KPIs

Content marketing costs are approximately 60-65% less than other forms of marketing and generates 3 times as many leads for every dollar spent. Many successful brands spend a minimum of 40% of their marketing budget on producing and distributing content.

Choosing the most effective key performance indicators to measure the success of your content marketing strategy is not simple. Measuring the right KPI helps you to evaluate which tactics are and aren't working.

The Key Steps in the KPI Process:

1. *Identify* your relevant KPIs.
2. *Create* scorecards.
3. *Evaluate* how well your business goals are being met.
4. *Change* strategies and processes as needed.

The most common KPIs for content marketing are to increase a) brand awareness, b) social engagement, c) network quantity, and d) leads/sales. As well as decrease sale conversion rates, boost click-through rates, increase and calculate cost per click.

Although the content marketing KPIs are some of the common, straightforward, easy to monitor, track, and measure with any of the numerous analysis tools; this doesn't mean you need to limit yourself to the above only. Identify the most relevant KPIs tomeasure your success in managing your KPI.

Every business has its own personality. Therefore, it's essential to track KPIs that are relevant to growing your brand. Without focus,you want to know if your marketing efforts are effective. Don't spend unnecessary time, energy or money doing what isn't driving results.

Measuring performance is not all numbers; it's also understandingthe process of how your consumer clients and customers make purchasing decisions. How can content marketing affect your changes to influence brand choice?

Let's look at the most useful quantitative brand metrics.

1 Awareness. What do you want your potential customers to

remember about your brand? Rank by importance for you. TOMA, top-of-mind awareness, creates spontaneous brand awareness or promoted brand awareness.

2. Familiarity. What do you want potential clients to know and recognize about you? Is there TOMA for you in a specific area, ranked by importance, brand salience, and strength of distinctive brand assets?
3. Consideration. What do you want to know? KPI importance, purchase intent.
4. Purchase. What do you want to find out? KPI's importance, sales volume and sales value.
5. Advocacy. Would your customers recommend your brand to their friends? Net Promoter Score (NPS)

STEP 4

Know Your Audience(s)

Your audience is online, in the billions: but how do you separate the signal from the noise? You do that by knowing your audience and demonstrating that knowledge. Once you have an idea of what, how, and when to communicate your message, you should figure out what content and messages people care about. Before you start writing, you must know the intended audience. Here's how:

Understand your target market, the current market, and your position. Your content must address all three simultaneously. In addition to the questions about how to identify your target market, start asking yourself what problems your company's product or service solves? What does the target audience stand to gain from choosing my product or service? To create a sound USP statement or audience definition, you want to be able to address what your product or service is. Also, fully understand the purpose of your content goal, the mission.

Raechelle-ism: If you provide insurance as a service, don't sell, "Pre-planning for peace of mind in times of tragedy." Consider your target audience, (ex. Your target a young family to address their fear of loss. Try a positioning statement such as, "I provide financial security in times of great uncertainties for [young families] when the unknown is the last thing we should have to focus on [insert below virtual through storytelling or visual communications."

A good positioning statement

Template 1 - For [target market] who [statement of need] the [product or service] is a [type of product] that [key benefit]. Unlike [primary competitor], our product [differentiation statement]

Template 2 - [target market] the [brand, product or service] is the [differentiation statement] among all [type of product] because [key benefit].

This is one of two methods; a sound consistent strategy that supports people on each side of your product; people who are still deciding what their main challenges are, and people who are already using your product to overcome these challenges. Your content reinforces the solution(s) you are offering and makes your customers more qualified users of your product.

Discover all you can about YOUR audience. Remember, content is meant to be consumed. So, who are you creating yours for? This is true for both those that are starting out or veterans of marketing. By knowing your audience, you'll be able to produce more relevant and valuable content consumers will want to read and even share with others.

Are you focusing on a single demographic, or would you like to expand your message to attract many audiences? Keep in mind that even as your business relies on various and different customers, due to varied business offerings, your content strategy can cater to multiple audiences.

There's no one-size-fits-all for all companies. Your possible target audience, including various demographics (profiles), requires various content campaigns based on your goals. Using a varied style of content types and channels will ensure easier campaign customization and your delivery of different content to every kind of audience you have in mind. In addition, high visibility (possible response) and interaction with those your company does business with.

Who are you writing for, your primary audience? Who is your secondary audience? [see the appendix for market segment chart] Remember your content casts a long shadow, a ripple effect. These are not those whose attention you intended to capture; however, they are affected by the message, service, or product solutions offered. Keep in mind to "speak to the pain and solve the problem." Ask yourself, why does this matter to the reader, what is the main concern, and how does the content prove that you have the solution(s).

Write for your audience. Consider your writer's voice, formal vs. informal, casual vs. professional, etc, the amount of detail, and how simple or complex the content should be. Not to mention the best media mix.

STEP 5

Access Your Current Position

To establish a solid creative approach for developing, implementing, maintaining, evaluating, and improving for the interest of your target market(s), a specific image uniquely different from the competition is imperative. To do so, you want to follow the following 3 steps. These steps will help to place you in the perfect position.

1. Select a position concept
2. Decide on a relevant marketing mix to convey your position
3. Design the features that convey your position.

The place or position you occupy in the minds of your audience and how it distinguishes you from your competitors is one of the most important marketing concepts. These concepts can broadly be classified into 3 types:

<u>Functional</u>: used when your brand provides solutions to problems and benefits to customers. The focus, the function, benefit, or utility provided to the customer

<u>Symbolic</u>: useful for creating a brand image that helps build brand equity, a sense of [social] exclusive relationship, and connectivity between the customer and your brand.

Experiential: created sensory and cognitive stimulation in the minds of the customer. The purest relatable experience for thecustomer.

Companies use a positioning process, which is a stepwise method, to place the product or service in the right way in the consumer's mind. If a company decides to change the way people perceive a brand, then they revamp the logo, slogan, etc. of that brand. This process is known as repositioning of the brand, which helps create a different image of that brand.

STEP 6

The Best Content Channels

Content Formats & Platforms.

What forms will your content take? Should it be in the form of infographics, videos, blog posts, podcasts, or vlogs? Having identified the topics you would like to focus on, you'll have to see which formats will allow you to best express that position. Just as you'll be able to create content in several formats, you'll have different channels you'll be able to publish too. Channels can include owned properties, like your website and blog, and social media properties, like Facebook and Twitter. Let's take a look at the social media content strategy step-by-step later. Content Management

Deciding how you'll create and publish all your content may be a frightening task.

The first, and perhaps most important step, is to choose the primary social media platforms you will focus on. Instead of trying to post on every social media platform out there, focus on the one or two that will have the most impact on your business.

To do this, you need to know your audience:

1. Where do they spend most of their time when it comes to social media?
2. Where do they like to interact with brands and businesses?
3. What sites influence them to purchase?
4. Who are the biggest influencers in your space and what platforms do they use?

Content strategy includes the understanding of who is responsible for creating what, where it is being published, when it is going live, and what you wish to accomplish with your social media campaign. Today's content strategies prevent clutter by managing content from a subject standpoint.

With the constant flow of content, news and ideas, it is easy to get lost in the day-to-day intricacies of managing multiple social media accounts. Live tweets for major events or reactive posts associated with significant news are engaging for your audience and interesting to create. However, you don't want to lose sight of the larger picture, which requires planning and sticking to a well-organized social media calendar centered on the content you recognized your audience is interested in.

A social media calendar will save time and permit you to trace and test different strategies to work out what resonates most with your audience. As a content strategy, both planning out a social calendar and scheduling posts in advance will prevent you from scouring trending topics and news stories each day searching for ideas. It will also build greater consistency in terms of your brand voice and elegance, as opposed to posting in a reactive or unplanned way.

When planning a content calendar around topics, you'll be able to easily visualize your company's message and assert yourself as an authority in your market over time. So, let's dive into the specific way to create a content marketing plan. *Plan, Schedule, Publish, Promote, Track, and Tweak your content.*

Facebook currently has over 3 billion daily active users. YouTube has over 2 billion active users. Instagram has over 1 billion. Twitter has almost 400 million, LinkedIn has approximately 790 million, Pinterest has 250 million TikTok has 1 billion active user monthly.

Why all these statistics about how many social media users there are?

To make one, powerful point: your customers and potential customers are DEFINITELY on at least one, if not more of these social media platforms. With such a staggering number of people using social media every single day, it is one of the most POWERFUL ways to grow your business. Social media platforms allow you to attract new customers and connect with audiences that you never would otherwise. And if your business isn't location-dependent, you can reach customers thousands of miles away through social media. You don't need to rely only on local customers. By posting on social media, you can even attract customers from other countries.

You can get your brand in front of a vast audience who might otherwise not hear of you. Through consistent posting on social media, you can build a powerful brand that separates you from the crowd. And you can establish yourself as a thought leader in your industry by regularly posting new, insightful content.

Of course, these realities also raise some important questions:

1. What is the best platform to use?
2. What tactics should you use to be seen by most people?
3. Are there certain types of content that perform better than others?
4. How can you regularly post content?
5. What etiquette rules do you need to follow?

Many business owners think that if they simply start posting on social media, they'll be successful and attract new customers. But it doesn't work this way. To build your business through social media, have a strategy in place.

Niche Relevant Content

You need to know where you're going to post, what you're going to post, how often you're going to post, and more. It's important to have a strategy for engaging with your audience. Simply put, you need to have a plan.

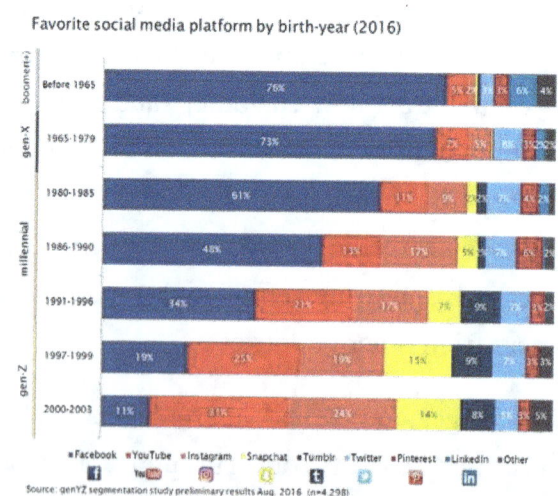

It's not enough to post across a variety of social media networks. Without a definitive plan for how you're going to use social media, you probably won't get your desired result. However, if you do have a plan, you'll find yourself quickly building an audience.

If your audience is younger, you may want to focus on Instagram, SnapChat, and YouTube If your focus is on business professionals, LinkedIn may be a good place to focus. If you're targeting Baby Boomers, FaceBook is probably a good place to start.

Keep in mind that you want to be where your audience is. You want to publish most of your content on the social media site where your audience hangs out the most. After all, you want your audience to interact with your content. If you publish primarily on platforms where they don't spend their time, they'll never engage with what you post.

If you don't know where your audience spends most of their social media time, simply ask them! Send out an email to your emaillist and ask them to tell you what social media platforms they use themost. Create a poll on several different social media sites and ask your followers to respond.

Asking is one of the most effective ways to find out where your audience spends their time. Another great way to determine where your audience spends their time is to look at the content you've already posted on social media and see what has gotten the biggest response. Have you gotten more comments, likes, and shares on oneparticular social media site? This is the one you want to focus on.

One other thing to consider when choosing your social media platform is what you're offering. Depending on the products or services you provide, one platform may be better than another. For example, if you sell physical products, a visual platform like Instagram or Pinterest might be the best option for you.

On the other hand, if you're primarily focused on selling services, a platform like Facebook, Twitter, or LinkedIn might work more effectively for you since you can explain a bit more about what you're selling.

As you consider which platform(s) to use, you must think smaller rather than bigger. You don't want to spread yourself too thin across multiple social media platforms. It would be better to focus on and master one or two platforms rather than to try to constantly post on ten different ones. The reality is that you probably don't have enough time to post across a variety of platforms. You will get better results if you give 100% of your energy to a few platforms instead of 25% of your energy to a bunch of different platforms.

If you're still not sure which platform to focus on even after surveying your existing audience, you can always fall back on Instagram/Facebook to start. With over 4 billion users combined, you can be sure that your target audience spends at least some time here.

At the end of the day, what matters most is not the particular platform you choose but rather that you choose and stick with it. When it comes to social media, consistency is almost always the most effective way to win an audience. Pick your platform and commit yourself to posting regularly on it.

STEP 7

Your Content Type

One of the most obvious roadblocks when considering a social media content calendar is knowing what to post. It would be overwhelming to turn up at your content meeting with enough ideas to fill a complete calendar, months ahead of time (your team might also urge you to get a cat, a hobby, *anything*). While a year-long schedule is a bit much, having a long-term social media plan *will* facilitate your set realistic goals and make the method of making a content calendar more manageable. Because there are always solutions to the toughest challenges, there are, of course, some strategies to make sure you never run out of things to speak about on social media. Don't depend on exciting things happening within your community or company to dictate what you post and when. Unless you are planning to make the 5 o'clock news yourself (not recommended. Law enforcement might not share your humor), there will be slow times and it is important to possess an inspiration to remain active on social media through these lean times.

Raechelle – ism, there are two kinds of content posted on social media: original and curated.

- Original content is content that you simply make to post on social media.
- Curated content gets shared from various sources around the web.

An ideal social media optimization strategy incorporates both kinds of content.

You can optimize this content through something as simple as testing your headlines. Since your audience sees your headlines first, when finding your content on social sites, you might want to experiment with different headlines to determine which of them resonate best with your audience.

It is valuable to possess multiple headlines for content; multiple headlines allow you to push an identical piece of content. It makes your content appear fresh, although it should be something you posted 12 hours (Note this is where I suggested wait time for 80% accuracy for a/b testing) prior. To get this process rolling, conduct a social media audit use things you have posted in the past thatreceived high engagement from your audience. To do this, you'll have to garner all your unique social media analytics from sources like Twitter or Facebook Insights. If you are employing a social media management tool, you'll find metrics across multiple social networks in one place. If you are just getting started with a social strategy or don't have old posts to analyze, do an audit of a competitor in your industry. Rummage around for hashtags or keywords in your trade and identify the accounts with the absolute best engagement.

Once you have some basic topics in mind, it helps to use a more in-depth social media tool, which manages, markets, schedules, etc.; all helping you pay close attention based on the algorithm and science behind the content that makes your audience tick. There are also tools which provide competitive research that reveals comprehensive view of hashtags, keywords, brands and topics that the audiences like yours and are engaging with on different social platforms. You'll use this information to craft posts that are highly relevant to your audience and expand your reach to others who might also be inquisitive about your content.

Content marketing <u>social media</u> is all about appealing to those who follow your brand and providing them with value. It is your responsibility to test different strategies and kinds of content to determine what your audience likes best. To achieve success with social media optimization, you need to continually evolve your strategy. While Mac N Cheese is good, you would get bored if that was the only thing on the menu every day. Content is evolving and changing, so you and your strategy must grow with it.

Like SEO, keywords play a vital role in your content strategy; you need to know what topics, keywords, and hashtags your audience uses to seek out information about your industry. Understanding how your audience searches on social media, you'll enhance your content strategy to drive more people to your page.

When you select keywords for your campaign, use content media-specific keyword tools. <u>People use different keywords on social media than they use while searching online</u>. If you don't know where to begin with keywords, try optimization in your searches for the perfect phrases for your campaign.

For instance, if you have a gym business, keywords would be "fitness," " CrossFit," or anything else you would want a reader to search for to find a service.

STEP 8

Your Content Calendar

Once you've optimized your social media profile, it's time to mapout how often you'll post, as well as what you'll post.

Ideally, you want to do this before you begin posting. This will help you map out exactly what, when and where you want to post. Consider creating a content media calendar in which you map out what you will post each day during a given period (week, month, year). This calendar will include what you're going to post, as well as when you'll post it.

Even if you've already started to post continue to pre-plan until you have a batch of posts with your clearly defined voice and call- to-action. When creating your content calendar, ask yourself these questions:

1. How often will you post? Ideally, post at least one piece of content once per day. This will keep your social mediaprofile active and show your followers that you're engaged on social media.
2. What sort of content will you post? Your goal/call to action (cta) will shape the types of content you share.

For example, if you're a life coach, you may want to regularly share inspirational quotes and photos. If you're a health practitioner, daily health tips could be incredibly helpful for your audience. When it comes to determining the types of content you're going to post, think of what will add the most value to your audience. WIIFT (what's in it for 'them') quick pro quo.

1. What formats will you use? The most effective businesses utilize a variety of formats on social media. In other words, they don't just post text. They also use images, videos, polls,

quizzes, and more. The more variety you use, the more you'll appeal to a wide range of individuals.

If you're struggling to figure out what to post, you may want to use a tool like Content Calendar. This will give you inspiration for every day of the year. It will also guide you as to what types of content might be most relevant depending on the time of year(holidays, seasons, etc.) and context.

You may be thinking: Why do I have to map all these out in advance? Why can't I just start posting? There are two reasons whyyou should utilize a social media calendar. The first is that it helps you to be consistent with your posting. One of the biggest challengesthat confront businesses when using social media is being consistent.

If you're not consistent, you can lose the attention of your audience. After all, there are millions of things being posted every single day. If you're not consistently posting, your audience will turn their attention elsewhere.

Marianne Litman says it like this: If your social media goes darkfor weeks at a time, you're not doing yourself or your followers anyfavors. Waiting weeks, or even days, between posts can kill off the enthusiasm you've built up. This can lead to an uninterested audience or people jumping ship completely and unfollowing you.

Once you have designed a concept regarding the kinds of contentyou would like to post, it is time to make a posting schedule. After auditing your past posts or competitors' posts, you'll begin to note trends. Pay careful attention to what days and times they were postedand on which platforms. Make a note of specific themes that naturally grab your attention; as a civilized spy, what grabs your attention is what has been grabbing the legitimate audiences', your community, or your ideal client.

This information will help you to organize and plan your posts to invite the most visibility. No one is suggesting plagiarism – you are better than that – but getting pointers about what works from an established campaign can only help you. Make a schedule that suits your workflow and keep it up. It could be that you have new work every Monday, Wednesday, and Friday, or perhaps you post your best work from the week on Sunday mornings. It doesn't need to be a huge undertaking; it just needs to be consistent.

By creating a social media calendar to complement your content calendar, you do the hard work of figuring out what you're going to post upfront. You take the guesswork away and ensure that you won't struggle to figure out what to publish.

This makes it much easier for you to be consistent over the long run since you don't have to constantly be trying to figure out what you're going to post.

Second, using a social media calendar "forces" you to be active on social media. You can't use the excuse of not knowing what to post. You've already laid out what you're going to post and it's important to stick to your schedule if you're going to win clients and influence markets.

Here are suggestions supported by the foremost up-to-date research on how often to post to every social media platform for optimum visibility:

- Facebook pages: 1-2 per day
- Twitter: 1-5 times per day
- Instagram: 3-7 times per day
- Instagram Stories: frequent times per day at least 2x daily

- Pinterest: 3-20 times per day
- LinkedIn: 1-5 times per week

Remember, only move to the recognized practices concerning the best times to post on each platform, dictated by specific industries and niches once you have developed consistency in posting. A general rule of thumb the best time to post on social media overall is Tuesday through Thursday at 9am or 10am; the worst day is Sunday. Posting frequently is a method to remain in front of your audience, but don't emphasize quantity over quality. Be wary of sharing content that is irrelevant or redundant just to fulfill a man-made posting quota.

Every audience is exclusive, which is why you may want to conduct an analysis and learn all about your audience as you manage your social media content calendar. Take a glance at your calendar and your analytics to seek out trends and patterns within the data. Noticing trends will tell you how people on different platforms react to different types of content and different posting times.

Don't get frustrated by creating a posting schedule that works will be a process of constant experimentation and refinement; this is a true example of "trial and error." In the end, this pays off not only with a social media content calendar that delivers results but also by helping you continually gain a much better understanding of what your audience is seeking. As you still fill in your social media calendar, fiddle with different posting times and the number of times per week you post. It will provide you with lots of insight into what works specifically for your audience.

Raechelle-ism, used the visit, engagement, and revenue (if available) stats from previous periods to assess which styles of content are most successful and perhaps replicated. To assist with writer's block, use the three Rs of a successful content marketing

strategy: Repurpose, Reuse, Recycle. If you have already published an in-depth blog with plenty of research and valuable information, this can be a good opportunity to repurpose this content by dividing it into smaller, pieces and publishing this information as a listicle or infographic! Be sure you incorp evergreen content as much as possible. Evergreen content will always be relevant in content marketing strategies. Carve out time to write down 10 or 20 timeless pieces that you simply can repost recycle when you don't have time to write something new. Content, typically, is barely seen by 10% of your followers, so if the content is timeless, the public won't know that this is second-hand content. The great thing about an honest piece of evergreen content is that it can successfully drive traffic and engagement for years. And if it ever becomes outdated? Just shine it up with a fast refresh and reuse it to your heart's content.

3rd PRINCIPAL

OPTIMIZE YOUR SOCIAL PERSONA

If you went to a business's social media page and saw that they didn't have a picture, barely had any information about their business, and weren't very active, would you want to connect with that business? Probably not. Therefore, you must optimize your social media profile. You want to make your profile as informative and attractive as possible. You want your profile to draw people in, not push them away.

As Itamar Gero says; *"Part of your lead generation effort involves building a strong social persona."* Once your social profile is up, potential clients are likely going to come across it - and not just current clients, but also anyone within their extended network.

The last thing you want is to have a social profile that's anything but presentable. So how do you optimize your profile? Here are some specific recommendations.

Select A Professional Username

Ideally, you want your username to be either your name or the name of your company. In other words, you don't want to create a username like KornOnTheJob@e-mail.com. This comes across as unprofessional and won't set you up for success.

Your username typically is also the URL of your social profile. For example, if your username is John Smith, your Facebook profile URL will be www.facebook.com/JohnSmith.

Ideally, you want to keep your username the same across all the social networks. This helps people find you on every social platform.

For Facebook, set up a professional page, not just a personal profile. In other words, set up a page that is dedicated solely to your business. You will only be posting business-related things on this page. No photos of your pets, nonsensible memes, or other unrelated items. You want to use your business page to build your brand.

However, if you use your personal page due to the professional connections and community you have fostered, continue to use it, but refrain from intermingling personal and professional.

High-Quality Profile Photo

Whether you're uploading a picture of yourself or your logo, use a high-quality photo. Ideally, the photo will have been professionally taken or the logo professionally designed. Be sure your photo is at least 300 pixels per inch (ppi). The photo is one of the first things that people see when they click on your social media profile. You want to put your best foot forward when it comes to your profile photo. If you need to have a logo designed, Fiverr and Upwork are great places to start. They make it incredibly easy to get a logo designed inexpensively.

A Compelling "About" Section

This section is where you tell the story of your business. It's where you communicate what you're all about and what matters most to you. Make your About Section both compelling and concise.

Depending on the social platform you use, you may have limited space to write about your information. In that case, try to get to the heart of what makes your business different from every other business. What is it that you do that sets you apart from everyone else? Include that information in your About section.

Also include links to your website, your other social media profiles, and any other relevant links. Make your About section as thorough as possible so that people get a good feel for what your business is all about. Remember to get to the point without being wordy. You do not want to lose them in too much detail.

Another sure way to capture the reader is with an attention-grabbing heading, [also good for content post and all copywriting] T.I.T.L.E.(S). This is a teaser, instruction, threat, list, engagement, and secret or a combination.

Professional Cover Photo

Almost every social media platform allows you to upload a cover photo. The cover photo spans the top of your social media profile and sits behind your profile photo. Like your profile photo, you want your cover photo to be as professional as possible. If your business has a slogan or motto, consider putting that slogan on your cover photo. If you don't have a slogan, you could feature a photo of your products. Ideally, you want your cover photo to further emphasize some element of your business.

Your Contact Information

Remember, you're trying to grow your reach and revenue. This means you want to make it as easy as possible for potential customers to contact you. In the Contact section, include as many ways as possible to contact you.

This can include your business phone number, email address, physical address, and any other possible ways to connect. You can also invite people to message you directly on the platform.

Resources to consider your social platform (and other landing pages), scheduling system, LinkedIn, Linktr.ee, and Hello, etc.

Professionalism

As you optimize your overall profile, think about how you want to represent yourself and your business online. Your social media profile will be the first touchpoint for some potential clients, and it's critical that your profile feels professional. If your social media profile isn't optimized and doesn't feel professional, there's a good chance you'll [or have] turn away potential clients.

This tends to defeat the first goal of content marketing strategy.

Use Hashtags

Hashtags are metadata tags used to enable cross-reference content, shared topics or themes.

For example:

- #theSolutionArchitect
- #KreativeInsights
- #realworldsolutions
- #brandstrategist
- #contentmarketingstrategy

Grouping posts by subject; if you add a hashtag to a post, it will be grouped with all other posts with the same hashtag.

If you see a post with a hashtag, you can click on that hashtag and see all the other posts with the same hashtag. For example, if you clicked on the hashtag #letstalkbranding, you would see all the other posts people had created about this topic if they used the #letstalkbranding hashtag. However, the more you use it and your audience connect with your post with it you begin to trend, draw more attention to your content.

Some sites, such as Twitter, highlight the most popular hashtags, giving you a sense of what's trending at any given time.

You can also follow hashtags so that you regularly see posts with a given hashtag.

The power of hashtags is that they allow you to get your content in front of a broader audience. In other words, you can have your posts seen by more than just your followers. By adding the appropriate hashtags, you can get them seen by thousands, if not millions of others.

How exactly do you use hashtags? Typically, you create a social media post. At the end of the post, you add a hashtag that is somehow related to the post. For example, let's say someone is seeking tips related to content marketing or branding strategy, they would seek outposts with the hashtags related to #contentmarketingstrategy, #brandmarketing, #brandstrategy, #marketingandadvertising, etc. In creating your content, you would do the same, using relevant hashtag(s) to the content you're posting. It might look something like this:

Before you do launch your campaign, spend at least ten minutes searching relevant hashtags. Notice that you can add multiple hashtags to a post. Depending on the platform you're using, you may be limited by space in terms of how many hashtags are appropriate.

One thing to be careful about. If your hashtags aren't related to the content of your post, there's a chance you could turn people away from you. Keep in mind when using hashtags, you don't want hashtags to dominate the post. The best practice is to place them toward the end of a post unless you can sensibly place them within the post.

For example, if you attach a #letstalkbranding hashtag to a completely unrelated post about a coffee shop you like, some people won't like it and will feel like you're "abusing" hashtags. As much as possible, keep your hashtags closely related to the content you're posting.

Many websites can help you find the right hashtags to use with your social media posts, such as:

- All Hashtag [https://all-hashtag.com/hashtag- generator.php]
- SeekMetrics [https://seekmetrics.com]

- Hashtag Generator [https://hashtagsgenerator.net]

4th PRINCIPAL

AWARENESS & VISIBILITY

Once you've created your social media content calendar and optimized your profile, it's time to begin posting content to social media. This is where the rubber meets the road. It's time to start putting out valuable [content] on your chosen social media channels. What sort of content should you be posting? If you want to win new clients and satisfy your existing ones, establish yourself as an influencer, it's essential to post content that will add value to your audience.

Again, you're not just posting to post. This is a critical point. Rather, you're trying to provide your audience with high-value information that will help them live their best life possible. Each post should be helpful in some way to your audience. How do you do this?

- Have them think about something in a new way
- Want to act like they never have
- Laugh or smile
- Learn and share something valuable

This goes back to knowing your audience. If you know your audience well, you know what they will find most valuable. If you don't know your audience, you'll struggle to post things that resonate with them.

Consider posting things like:

- Written for the reader
- Content that invokes emotion
- Enlighten through humor
- Inspire them with inspiration
- Education as well as entertain
- Tell a story
- Open-ended content
- Real-time updated content
- Visual content
- Live streaming

When creating your content calendar and posting on social media, constantly ask yourself the following question:

1. Is this adding value to my audience?
2. If it is, then post it. If you don't think it will add much value to your audience, don't post it, return later with fresh eyes.
3. If you're not sure which types of content add the most value to your audience, try experimenting with different formats. You might find that videos performs better than photos, or that your audience likes tutorials and tips.

Test out a variety of formats and see which ones resonate most with your audience and with what type of content. You may be thinking: I don't have time to constantly be posting! The good news is that you don't have to be on all the different social media platforms all day every day. Using a tool like Buffer or Hootsuite, you can schedule out weeks, or even months, of posts in advance.

Remember that these are not the only channels; it's up to you to decide which media mix you'll use, and the frequency in which you'll use them. Then, sit down with yourself and ask the following:

1. Where do I want to engage the audience?
2. Where do I want them to land (to ultimately learn about the offer)?
3. How many person(s) will be a part of this and what are their roles?
4. How will I communicate the offer (in one-two sentence(s), think explaining something to a 5th grader)?
5. As a business, where am I going (the mission statement)?
6. As a business, what do we do (your story in 3 to 5 sentences, again, think of that 5th grader)?
7. What is the business' key goal this year?
8. What are the three measurable steps that you'll take that will help you reach your goal?
9. How will you measure each step? The Metric? Number? Frequency?
10. What were the 1st, 2nd and 3rd place goals that followed your top goal for this year?*

This will be New Year's contenders.

Consider using your social media calendar in conjunction with one of the many social scheduling tools or the built-in scheduling functions on any of the social media channels you frequently use. By scheduling a significant number of social media posts in advance, you can save yourself hours.

Engage With Your Followers

It's not enough to simply post on social media and then go on your way. The real power of social media is that it creates conversations between you and your followers. At least, it should create conversations. Conversations are the key to getting more clients through social media. It's important to engage with your followers regularly and consistently by responding to comments, answering questions, solving challenges, and more.

Social media is not a one-way street. Rather, it's a conversation between you and those who follow you. A conversation involves both speaking (posting) and listening (responding).

If you want to build relationships and gain clients through social media, you need to apply the conversational approach (having conversations or responding to your audience), not just publish new content.

One of the things that matter most when it comes to social media authenticity is that you don't want to come across as a huge corporation that only posts on social media and never engages in conversation. Instead, you want to authentically engage with your followers. *Attraction is authenticity and authenticity equals attraction.* It will attract new followers and turn them into new clients.

Another reason to engage with followers is that social media platforms tend to prioritize the posts with the most engagement. The posts with the most likes, comments, shares, and overall engagement get shown more frequently than those posts with very little engagement.

If you want to get your posts seen by as many people as possible, then you absolutely must engage with your followers regularly.

Note: Take advantage of Push Notification or set a time to respond. Type responses to 33-50% or more of commentor (and "Likes" Be sure to use 4-5 words or more. Emojis do not count!!

Raechelle-ism, respond with five words or more to drive the algorithm in the favor of your post. If you like to use emojis, understand they are not counted as characters, so are not counted as responses.

You must:

1. Talk with your followers
2. Create conversations
3. Answer questions
4. Respond to any problems that are raised

Rather than talking to your audience, your goal is to talk with them, as much as possible, and create real relationships with them. There is no revenue without a relationship. Conversation builds trust.

What are some ways that you can create conversations with your followers?

- Ask questions.
- Do live videos in which you talk directly with your audience.
- Conduct polls/surveys
- Ask people to comment on a particular subject.
- Make statements that will get people talking (just be careful about being too controversial).

Focus on being as real as possible on social media and you're guaranteed to create conversations with your followers.

Follow The Right People

Social media isn't just about getting people to follow you. It's also about following the right people and having conversations with them.

Consider following influencers in your industry.

For example, if you're a financial adviser, follow other financial advisers in your industry. If you're a life coach, try to connect with other life coaches. If you're in the health and wellness space, follow other health and wellness practitioners.

Once you've started following them, interact with the material they share. Comment on it, repost it and share it with your followers. Try to develop relationships with others and simply be part of the conversation that's happening.

Additionally, consider being part of groups that are related to your industry. Both Facebook and LinkedIn have robust group features, and there are millions of groups on every subject imaginable.

- Join the groups.
- Engage in conversation.
- Try to help others.
- Be a useful resource.

One note of importance regarding groups is that you must be very careful about promoting yourself and your services in groups. Many groups have strict rules about this kind of thing. When you join a group, focus on adding value, not promoting yourself. The more value that you add, the more you'll become known as an expert in your industry. This will naturally attract clients to you. Look for the gaps and fill the void (i.e. sell the pain and solve the solution).

As you follow influencers in your industry and take part in groups, take note of the valuable information that others are sharing. What sorts of posts do others share that resonate deeply with you? What content adds the most value to you?

Additionally, what sort of content seems to get the best response?

What posts generate the most conversations and engagement?

This is the kind of content that you want to be sharing with your audience. You don't have to be completely original with what you share online. Don't be afraid to adopt techniques and strategies that are working well for others. But do it in your voice and tone. Your audience wants to hear and see you. Also give credit where credit is due. If a technic of process, you share is courtesy of another give mention to your inspiration.

In addition to joining online groups, several platforms focus heavily on answering questions that are posed by users. For example, Quora lets any user post a question and then other users try to answerthat question.

Quora is a great place to show off your expertise without being overly promotional.

It lets you speak directly to a person's challenges, offer helpful advice and answers, and build relationships online. If you do it rightand add a large amount of value to those on the platform, it can certainly lead to more clients.

It's also a great place to find frequently asked questions and postthem on your platforms for conversation and a way to add value by providing answers, tips, tools, or techniques on the topic.

5th PRINCIPAL

DISTRIBUTION AND MARKETING

he secret to success is creating content that appeals to your customers. How frequently is the necessity of sharing and promoting material overlooked in marketing? After all, your audience will not stumble across your content by chance. You must communicate your material to your target audience for it to be effective. A content distribution plan will assist you in successfully distributing and marketing content. Your content distribution strategy is your approach for getting your content in front of your target audience through multiple marketing channels, as mentioned in the previously.

Now that you've created your approach, it's time to determine the channels through which you'll disseminate your content. Content distribution channels, according to HubSpot, are the channels via which you share and market the content you create. Depending on your audience and resources, you'll use a different collection of channels to distribute your content.

The three most common forms of distribution channels are owned, earned, and paid. All three types cross paths with one another. To maximize their efficacy and achieve your company's goals, you can employ one or all the channels.

To help you enhance your content marketing, let's look at 15 content distribution platforms and the best strategies for increasing traffic from each.

Owned Media Channels

The channels that your company owns are known as owned media. Simply put, these are your channels, and you have complete control over the stuff you share. It covers your company's website, blog, social media profiles, email newsletters, and any other content you own. It may even be your own publishing mobile app.

Owned channels are the simplest kind of distribution because they involve the least amount of work. However, as previously stated, if you do not encourage your audience to your website, they will not be able to find your content. So, these are the most common and easiest strategies to get clients to read your material on owned media outlets.

#1 Website/blog

#2 Email newsletters

#3 Ebooks

#4 Infographics

#5 Video

Earned Media Channels

Earned channels are also called "shared" channels, i.e., earned media involve others sharing your content. This can take the form of guest posts, media coverage, and more. The key point of these channels is that anyone who shares your content does it for free— hence the name "earned".

Being promoted and recommended through earned media is one of the hardest things to achieve—though the most valuable due to its credibility and potential reach. Whether your content is shared by users or by brands, it will help your business thrive. While it requires a lot of effort from you, the amount of trust placed in these recommendations is huge.

#6 Guest blogging

#7 Press releases

#8 Social media groups

#9 QA Platforms

#10 Online platforms

#11 Podcasts

Paid Distribution Channels

Paid channels cover media that require payment for content distribution. Typically, they include pay-per-click (PPC) advertising, paid influencer content, sponsored content, and social ads.

Generally, earned media dominates overpaid distribution. However, this depends on your business niche and goals. Some companies prefer to choose paid distribution channels as their primary way of distributing content, while others stick to earned media channels.

#12 Pay-per-click (PPC) advertising

#13 Paid influencer marketing

#14 Sponsored content

#15 Paid social ads

#16 Distribute Your Content Effectively

Creating amazing content is just the first step. To share your content effectively, drive your leads and engage your audience. Content distribution channels will help you with that. If chosen correctly, they will boost your brand's awareness, help you find loyal followers, and encourage your readers to click, act, and becomeyour customers.

6th PRINCIPAL

SEO

on't look at your social media calendar as just a mere planning tool; as the simplest way to trace and measure campaigns across every platform you utilize, your calendar also works as a treasure map. Analyze the data you collect from your social media campaigns and optimize your social media calendar in the future.

As the easiest way to show how your business will produce at any given time, and while painless to make, it has proven notoriously difficult for novice content marketing strategists to remain true to the posting schedule. Nonetheless, give yourself some grace, you'lluse it to not only keep yourself organized but to reflect on how wellyour message is being received, how your brand is spreading, how your product and/or service is flourishing and where improvementsmay be made. Each time you map forward, track progress or evaluate success. Although not desired, slippage is expected. Minimize its occurrence.

At the starting line, brainstorm content that matches your brand and niche, create a content calendar for up to a few weeks to 6 months and use the primary month to check your content (watch for an increase in your social media optimization, SMO and social media analytics).

Quality content is very important, but it does not mean much to your business if your visitors and viewers don't convert into customers. Therefore, the art of analytics is so important -- by carefully monitoring, tracking, watching, and reporting on the numbers, you'll be ready to gauge what is working, what is not, and what can be improved.

Traffic is especially important, but it is vital your concentration on conversion rates. Perhaps your Instagram account only has 1,000 followers -- alternatively, your blog has 7,000 readers. However, your Instagram page contains a conversion rate of seven percent, and your blog only converts at about .01. This could tell you that, while your blog is particularly important for an initial introduction to your business, your Instagram is critical for sales, and should not be ignored.

Additionally, that specialization in analytics will aid you while refining and improving your strategy for the long haul. For instance, you notice your blog readers are particularly fascinated by your blogs that are associated with e-commerce, that information is important, as this could help direct your future strategy you'll now know to focus more heavily on e-commerce topics, which is then able to increase traffic (signaling your readers are pleased with your content) and ensure you are spending time and energy where it matters.

Raechelle-ism *Color-code content for simple usage and SMO re-usage. Consider including a long-form blog, SlideShare presentation, syndication content, daily comments, weekly (daily) videos, bi-weekly infographics/listicles, and monthly eBook.*

7th PRINCIPAL

PUTTING IT ALL TOGETHER

f you truly want to succeed on social media, you'll need to experiment to see what works best.

Different types of content will resonate with your audience. You may find that videos work well while inspirational quotes don't perform as well. Or you may find that asking questions generates discussions, but polls fall flat.

Experimentation is especially critical since social media platforms are constantly changing.

Currently, Facebook gives preference to posts that keep people on their site, such as videos. These posts show up in people's news feeds more often. Facebook doesn't give nearly as much exposure to posts that send people off their website, such as links. But this could change. In the future, Facebook may give preference to some other type of content.

The moral of the story.

Constantly test to see what works most effectively.

As you test, you'll discover what adds the most value to your audience. Then you can post more of this type of content, which will generate significantly more engagement. It ends up being a virtuous cycle that helps you connect with more and more people on social media.

DON'T WAIT ANY LONGER!

f you're not regularly using social media to build your business, you should be. The advantages of using social media are enormous. With social media you can:

- Attract new clients
- Build your brand
- Establish yourself as a thought leader
- Connect with new audiences
- Create meaningful relationships
- Connect with other influencers
- And so much more

Thankfully, it's not particularly complicated to get started building your social media awareness and creating your content marketing strategy as laid out in this step-by-step book.

You don't need to be intimidated. Even if you've never consistently posted on a platform, you can get started today. You can easily start building your business through the power of content. So, don't wait any longer. There are clients out there just waiting for you to find them.

BONUS PAGES

Grow Your Business Using Social Media

DR(HC) RAECHELLE RAE JOHNSON

Growing Your Business Using Social Media
Everything You Need to Know

The Impact of Social Media on Our Culture

In the present day, Facebook has more than 2 billion users who log in at least once every day. Many people (about 2 billion) check out YouTube frequently. To put it another way, there are a billion people on Instagram. About 330 million individuals use Twitter, while 303 million use LinkedIn and 250 million use Pinterest.

If you want to reach your current and future consumers, you must be present on at least one of these social networking networks. In order to reach more people, your business should take use of social media because of the sheer number of individuals that use it on a daily basis.

Through social media, businesses may reach new audiences and connect with potential customers. In addition, if your company's success isn't based on its physical location, you can promote to clients in other nations, even if they are thousands of miles away. And you can become a recognized authority in your field.

It's a common misconception among business owners that simply joining social media and promoting their company there will bring in new clients. However, that option does not exist here. Having a plan for communicating with your target demographic is vital if you want to expand your business via social media.

Just posting on various social media networks isn't enough. While social media has the potential to be a useful resource, without first developing a plan of attack, you may not achieve the desired outcomes.

Stage 1: Selecting Your Platforms

Instead of trying to make an impact on every possible social media platform, narrow your efforts to just one or two.

If you want to succeed at this, it's imperative that you understand your target market.

To what social media platforms do they devote much of their time?

If you want to know where people prefer to engage with brands and businesses, ask them this question:

Where do they go to get persuaded to make a purchase?

What social media sites do the most influential people in your field frequent?

Follow your target market. Use the social media platform where your target audience spends the most time publishing the bulk of your content. After all, you want people to engage with what you're putting out there.

It's best to ask your target market directly where they spend much of their time on social media if you're unsure. Send an email out to your contact list and inquire as to which social media sites they frequent most. Put together a poll for your followers to answer and share it across multiple platforms.

Looking at the content you've already posted on social media to see what has gotten the biggest response is another great way to figure out where your audience spends their time.

When deciding which social media platform to use, you should also think about the products or services you're peddling. It's possible that one platform is more suitable than another for your business than the others are, depending on the goods and services you're peddling.

In deciding which platform(s) to employ, it is crucial that you focus on the details rather than the big picture. You shouldn't dilute your efforts by promoting them equally across a number of different social media sites.

Instead of trying to maintain a presence on ten different sites, it's more effective to master just one or two. As opposed to spreading your efforts thin across several different platforms, it is more efficient to focus all of your efforts on a select few.

Ultimately, it doesn't matter which platform you pick so much as the fact that you pick one and stick with it. Keeping up a steady presence on social media is the best bet for attracting followers.

Stage 2: Optimizing Your Social Media Presence

You'll have more success if you focus on just one or two social media platforms rather than trying to dominate them all.

Successful completion of this task requires a thorough familiarity with the intended audience.

Which sites do they use the most?

This is the question you should ask consumers to learn more about how they interact with brands and companies.

If they need to be convinced to buy something, where should they go?

How often do the most influential people in your field use social media?

Focus on what your target audience wants. Publish the bulk of your content on the social media site where your ideal readers spend the most time. After all, your goal is for people to interact with your content.

If you aren't sure where your target audience spends much of their time on social media, simply ask them. Ask your email list's recipients which social networks they use most frequently by sending out a survey. Create a poll and disseminate it across all your channels to get feedback from your audience.

Finding out where your audience spends their time can also be aided by analyzing the performance of your previous social media posts to determine which types of content were most well received.

Think about the goods and services you're peddling when deciding which social media network to focus on. Depending on what you're selling, some platforms may be better suited to your business than others.

In determining which platform(s) to employ, it is vital that you focus on the minutiae rather than the overall picture. You shouldn't dilute your efforts by marketing them equally throughout a variety of various social networking networks.

Instead of trying to maintain a presence on ten different sites, it's more productive to master just one or two. As opposed to spreading your efforts across a lot of various platforms, it is more efficient to focus all your efforts on a select handful.

Ultimately, it doesn't matter which platform you pick so much as the fact that you pick one and stick with it. The greatest way to gain followers is to have an active social media profile.

Stage 3: Scheduling Your Posts is The Phase of Business

Planning your posting schedule and content strategy is the next step after polishing your social media presence.

Creating a "social media calendar" allows you to plan out what you will post on each site daily for a given time period (week, month, year). You can schedule not just when and what you'll post, but also how often, in this section. When planning your social media posts, consider the following questions:

How frequently will you be posting new information? It is recommended that you publish new content daily. By maintaining a current profile, you may demonstrate to your followers that you are making use of social media.

So, what exactly are you going to be committing to? The nature of your business will shape the types of material you choose to release. Focusing on delivering high-quality material that your audience can use is key to increasing engagement.

Please tell me about the file types you want to employ. The most prosperous businesses use numerous social media platforms. The use of any and all forms of communication technology (print, video, audio, kinetic, etc.) is commonplace.

If you're having difficulties coming up with material for your social media accounts, the PLR.me Social Media Calendar will help. As a result, you'll have something to look forward to every day of the year.

Two reasons why you should use a social media calendar are as follows:

To begin, it guarantees that you will never be late with a post again. Discontinuity is a significant challenge for social media managers running a business.

Keep in mind that a social media calendar "forces" you to remain active on several platforms. You can't make up an excuse about not knowing what constitutes proper material.

Stage 4: Start Sharing Content on Social Media

If you've taken the time to create a social media content calendar, it's now time to start distributing that content. Consistently providing valuable information to your audience is an excellent way to draw in new business and retain existing patrons.

You aren't just filling up the thread with meaningless text. Instead, you should focus on providing your audience with information that will genuinely help them. Your readers should learn something from each and every one of your posts.

Every piece you write ought to be geared toward helping your audience in some way.

- Just think about it from a different angle
- Perform like they've never done it before
- Expressing joy or a smile
- Education with Added Value
- Things you could talk about include
- Inspirational Quotes

Strategies and Hints that Can Help

Explanations in Video Form

Streaming videos that are current at the time of viewing
Influencing your audience using eye-catching imagery

And further

If you're filling up a content schedule or posting updates on social media, you should be asking yourself, "Is this bringing value to my audience?" Feel free to disseminate it if so. If you don't think it will engage or educate your audience, don't post it.

Experiment with different types of content to see what resonates most with your target demographic. There's a chance that you'll discover that video works better than images or that people appreciate how-tos and walkthroughs.

Now, you may be thinking, "I don't have time to always be blogging!" Using a scheduling program like Buffer or Hootsuite, you can prepare your social media posts weeks or even months in advance.

Stage 5: Communicate with Your Audience

Value in social media comes from the conversations you have with your target demographic. At the very least, it should spark some heated discussions. Conversation is the best technique to acquire new clients on social media.

Keep up a constant rate of conversation with your viewers. Keep the dialogue going by addressing people's comments, questions, and problems.

Connecting with people and drawing in new business on social media requires holding meaningful conversations, not just posting new content. Communication with your audience should be sincere. One of the most attractive qualities is honesty. Potential new followers will be drawn, and ultimately turned into paying patrons.

Social media networks give more weight to content that has garnered a lot of comments and shares, so it's crucial to interact with your audience. Posts that have a lot of interaction will be shown more frequently than those that don't.

How can you initiate dialogue with your fan base?

Questions are the key to unlocking knowledge.

Use real-time video streaming to engage with your audience.

Conduct a survey.

Try asking for their thoughts on something to get them involved.

Get what you want by writing comments certain to start a debate (just be careful about being too controversial).

Keep your social media posts as honest and open as possible, and you'll quickly find yourself engaging with a loyal following.

Stage 6: Adhere to the Right Leaders

Consider influential figures in your area and start learning from them. Financial professionals, for example, would do well to take their colleagues' advice. Connect with others who share your interest in life coaching.

It's only courteous to comment or like posts by people you follow on social media. Give it a response, share it with your followers, and make it viral. Engage them in conversation and introduce yourself.

You should also consider becoming a member of professional organizations. The fact that Facebook and LinkedIn both have millions of groups dedicated to every conceivable interest area attest to the value of their group functions. If you want to get the most out of your membership in a group, it's best to contribute to it rather than just take.

You can learn a lot about your area by connecting with other individuals who work in it and paying attention to what they contribute. Which of the things other people post most deeply affects you? In other words, this is the kind of content that should be shared with your intended audience.

Many websites exist only for the purpose of helping people with the issues they've brought up in online discussion boards. Anyone, for instance, can use Quora to pose a topic and receive feedback from the community.

Stage 7: Hashtags

With the help of hashtags, posts can be organized into groups discussing similar themes. The inclusion of a hashtag in a post will group that post with others that use the same hashtag.

If a post you're reading has a hashtag in it, clicking on that hashtag will take you to a feed of all other posts with that hashtag. Some social media platforms, like Twitter, highlight the most popular hashtags, making it simple to know what's popular at any given time. A user can also choose to "follow" a hashtag in order to be alerted whenever new material is published that uses that hashtag.

Using hashtags helps your content reach a wider audience. Your posts could be seen by tens of thousands more people if you use the appropriate hashtags.

Why do people usually use hashtags? The events typically unfold like this. Create something to share on one of your social media sites. Including a hashtag at the end of your article will increase its discoverability.

Before commencing any Crossfit workout, it is recommended that you spend at least 10 minutes warming up and stretching. CrossFit, CrossFit Workout, and CrossFit Lifestyle are all hashtagged.

Keep in mind a post may be ignored if the hashtags used have nothing to do with the content of the post. Always use appropriate hashtags while posting online.

Stage 8: A New Experiment

If you want to find true success on social media, you need to experiment to find out what methods are most effective. Numerous content styles will be well-received by your intended audience. Motivational sayings might not work as well as videos, yet videos could prove to be helpful.

The ever-changing landscape of social media makes experimenting essential. Facebook presently prioritizes material like videos that can maintain user interest. This, however, may be changing soon. In the future, Facebook may give certain types of posts more exposure.

Always conduct experiments to determine the efficacy of your hypotheses. Find out which of your posts your audience enjoys reading the most. Then you can upload similar content more often to see a surge in engagement. It creates a self-sustaining cycle that helps you meet more people and broaden your circle of contacts.

www.ingramcontent.com/pod-product-compliance
Lightning Source LLC
Chambersburg PA
CBHW070310220526
45465CB00004B/1826